On the Front Lines

The U.S. Army at War

by Terri Sievert

Consultant:

Thomas J. Evelyn
Lieutenant Colonel, Aviation
U.S. Army

CAPSTONE
HIGH-INTEREST
BOOKS

an imprint of Capstone Press
Mankato, Minnesota

Capstone High-Interest Books are published by Capstone Press
151 Good Counsel Drive, P.O. Box 669, Mankato, Minnesota 56002
http://www.capstone-press.com

Library of Congress Cataloging-in-Publication Data
Sievert, Terri.
    U.S. Army at war/by Terri Sievert.
    p. cm.—(On the front lines)
    Includes bibliographical references and index.
    ISBN 0-7368-0922-8
    1. United States. Army—Juvenile literature. 2. United States.
Army—History—20th century—Juvenile literature. [1. United States.
Army.] I. Title. II. Series.
UA25 .S55 2002
355'.00973—dc21   2001000446

Summary: Provides an overview of the U.S. Army, its mission, members,
history, recent conflicts, and modern equipment.

Editorial Credits
Blake Hoena, editor; Karen Risch, product planning editor; Steve Christensen,
    cover designer and illustrator; Katy Kudela, photo researcher

Photo Credits
Defense Visual Information Center, cover, 4, 6, 8, 10, 13, 14, 16, 20, 23, 24,
    27, 28

1 2 3 4 5 6 07 06 05 04 03 02

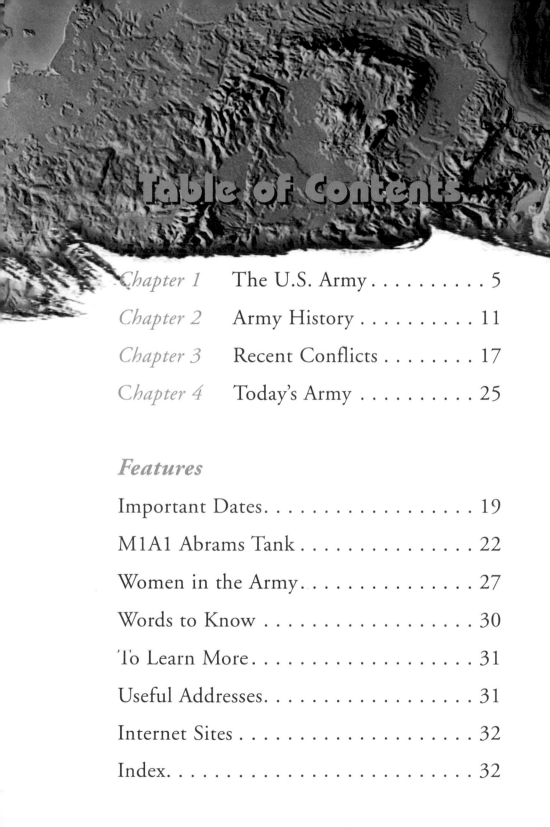

Table of Contents

CHAPTER 1

Learn about:

- The Army's mission

- Army members

- Army jobs

U.S. Army troops used tanks to attack Iraqi forces during the Gulf War.

The U.S. Army

In 1990, the Middle East country of Iraq invaded Kuwait. U.S. leaders wanted to free Kuwait from Iraqi control. They sent troops to the area. These events led to the Gulf War (1991).

On February 24, 1991, U.S. soldiers drove tanks into Iraq and Kuwait. This action began the ground war against Iraqi forces.

Sand storms prevented the tank drivers from seeing clearly. But the drivers found their way with the help of satellites. These spacecraft orbit Earth. The satellites sent signals to the tank drivers. The signals showed them where enemy forces were located.

The attack surprised Iraqi troops. U.S. forces destroyed many Iraqi tanks. Thousands of Iraqi soldiers surrendered to U.S. forces. The ground war ended after only four days of fighting.

Army members defend the United States on land.

The Army's Mission

The soldiers who drove the tanks into Iraq were members of the U.S. Army. The Army defends the United States on land.

U.S. military leaders often send Army members to different places around the world. Army members help keep peace in some areas. Some Army members are stationed in South Korea. They help guard the border between North Korea and South Korea.

Army members also have been sent to the country of Yugoslavia. In 1991, fighting broke out when this country split into several smaller republics. These countries include Croatia, Bosnia-Herzegovina, and Slovenia. Army members helped keep peace in the area.

The Army also helps people hurt by natural disasters such as floods and tornadoes. In 1998, Hurricane Mitch struck the Central American country of Honduras. Army engineers helped provide drinking water and rebuild schools. Army medical teams cared for sick and injured people. Army members also helped provide people with food and shelter.

Artillery troops fire missiles at enemy targets.

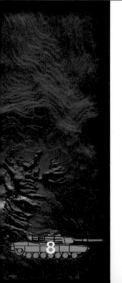

Army Members

People volunteer to serve in the U.S. military.
People who join the Army can be enlisted
members or officers. Officers have more training
than enlisted members. Officers direct enlisted
members in their duties.

Almost 500,000 people are active members of the U.S. Army. Active members work full time in the Army.

More than 550,000 people serve in the Army Reserves. Reserve members work part time in the Army. They train one weekend a month and serve two full weeks each year. Reserve members can be called to active duty in emergencies.

Army Jobs

Army members perform many duties. Some gather information about enemy forces. Others organize troops and supplies. Artillery troops launch rockets and missiles at enemy targets. Helicopter pilots carry supplies and soldiers where they are needed. Infantry troops fight on foot. Army engineers build roads and canals.

Some Army members receive special training. Army Rangers train to sneak into enemy areas. They then gather information about enemy forces. Paratroopers train to use parachutes. They use these strong, lightweight pieces of fabric to jump out of airplanes. Parachutes allow paratroopers to land safely on the ground.

CHAPTER 2

Learn about:

- Continental Army

- Early wars

- World wars

The Continental Army fought to gain freedom for the American colonies.

Army History

On June 14, 1775, the Continental Congress created the Continental Army. George Washington commanded this army. The Army fought against Great Britain during the Revolutionary War (1775–1783). The Continental Army fought to free the American colonies from British rule.

Continental soldiers fought British troops with muskets. Soldiers had a difficult time hitting distant targets with these guns. Soldiers also had to reload muskets after every shot they fired.

U.S. and British soldiers attached bayonets to the end of their muskets. They used these metal blades in hand-to-hand combat.

In 1781, the British surrendered. The colonies had won their freedom. The colonies then became the United States of America. After the war, the Army helped protect settlers from American Indian attacks. The U.S. Military Academy was established at West Point, New York, in 1802. This school trains soldiers to be officers.

Early Wars

The United States also fought the British in the War of 1812 (1812–1815). British naval officers were forcing U.S. sailors to serve on British ships. The British also were preventing the United States from trading overseas.

In the early 1800s, Great Britain had one of the most powerful militaries in the world. Neither the United States nor Great Britain was able to win the War of 1812. But the U.S. military successfully defended the United States against Great Britain's military. This success gained the United States respect from other countries.

During the Civil War (1861–1865), Southern and Northern states fought against each other. Some soldiers used repeating rifles during this

The Northern states battled the Southern states during the Civil War.

war. These guns fired more than one shot before soldiers had to reload them.

In 1865, the Southern states surrendered to the Northern states. The Civil War helped end slavery. More than 500,000 soldiers died during the war.

World Wars

During World War I (1914–1918), the United States fought for the Allied forces. These countries included Great Britain and France. The Allied forces fought the Central Powers. These countries included Germany and Austria-Hungary.

During this war, soldiers fought from trenches. These ditches stretched nearly 600 miles

Tanks were first used during World War I.

(970 kilometers) across France and Belgium. Tanks were first used during this war. The Allied forces defeated the Central Powers in 1918.

In World War II (1939–1945), the Allied forces included the United States, France, Great Britain, and the Soviet Union. They fought against the Axis powers. These countries included Germany, Japan, and Italy.

The U.S. Army helped the Allied forces win this war. U.S. infantry soldiers fought Japanese soldiers in the jungles of Asia. Army tanks battled German tanks in North African deserts. Army soldiers parachuted behind enemy lines at Normandy, France.

Vietnam War

During the Vietnam War (1954–1975), the United States tried to protect South Vietnam from North Vietnam.

The U.S. Army faced guerrilla warfare during this war. North Vietnamese soldiers fought in small groups. They often attacked suddenly and unexpectedly. The U.S. Army developed special units to combat these fighting methods. Green Berets were trained to sneak into enemy areas to battle enemy soldiers.

CHAPTER 3

Learn about:

- The Gulf War

- Aid to Somalia

- U.N. forces in Kosovo

U.S. Army soldiers were sent to Saudi Arabia during the Gulf War.

Recent Conflicts

After World War II, the U.S. military continued to prepare for large wars. The military's main goal was to defend the United States from the Soviet Union. The Soviet Union opposed the United States in several conflicts. These conflicts included the Korean War (1950–1953) and the Vietnam War.

In 1991, the Soviet Union split into several smaller countries. Some of these countries include Russia, Lithuania, and Armenia. U.S. leaders did not feel that these countries were a great threat to the United States. The Army then prepared to be ready for smaller conflicts.

Since Vietnam, the United States has not been involved in a major war. But the Army has taken part in several smaller conflicts.

Gulf War

On August 2, 1990, Iraqi forces invaded the country of Kuwait. U.S. leaders wanted to help free Kuwait. They sent more than 500,000 troops to nearby Saudi Arabia.

The attack on Iraqi forces was called Operation Desert Storm. It began January 17, 1991. The U.S. military first attacked Iraq with bombs and missiles. These weapons destroyed Iraqi military buildings, power plants, and bridges.

The Army began the ground war February 24, 1991. Helicopter pilots flew troops and equipment into Iraq. Army members drove tanks into Iraq and Kuwait. Other Army members attacked Iraqi forces with artillery, rockets, and missiles. Paratroopers dropped into enemy territory. They captured an Iraqi air base. Special teams broadcast messages to enemy troops. The messages told Iraqi soldiers to surrender. Many Iraqi soldiers decided to give up fighting.

The United States and its allies destroyed 4,000 Iraqi tanks in the ground war. Allies are countries friendly with one another. About 60,000 Iraqi soldiers were captured. Many Iraqi defense systems also were destroyed.

Important Dates

1775—Continental Congress creates the Continental Army; George Washington is placed in command of the Army; the Continental Army fights the British in the Revolutionary War.

1802—The U.S. Military Academy is established in West Point, New York.

1812—War of 1812 begins; the U.S. military successfully defends the United States against a powerful British military.

1861—Civil War begins; Northern states fight against Southern states; the Northern states' victory helps end slavery.

1898—Spanish-American War begins.

1914—World War I begins; the United States enters the war in 1917.

1939—World War II begins; the United States enters the war in 1941.

1950—Korean War begins.

1954—Vietnam War begins; the United States starts sending troops to Vietnam in the early 1960s.

1991—Gulf War begins.

1992—Operation Restore Hope begins in Somalia.

1999—United Nations sends peacekeeping troops to Kosovo.

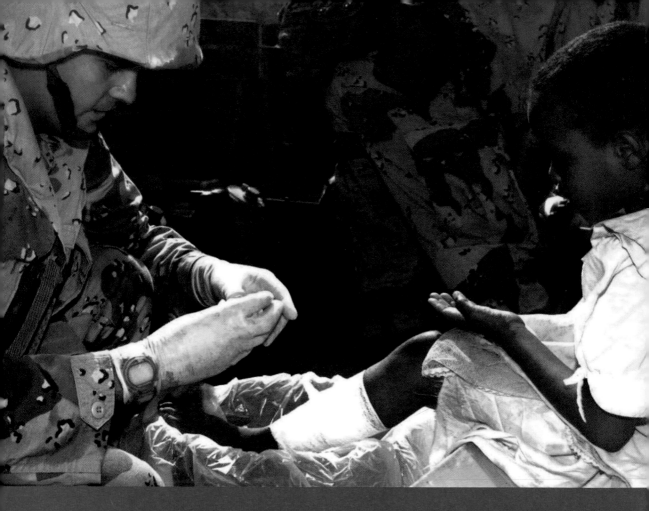

Army doctors helped care for sick Somalians during Operation Restore Hope.

Operation Restore Hope

In 1992, the U.S. military began Operation Restore Hope. During this mission, Army members helped people in Somalia receive food. Army doctors helped care for the sick.

Army members also had to protect food supplies from Somalian warlords. These military leaders often attacked and prevented the Somalian people from receiving food.

Peacekeeping Forces in Kosovo

The United Nations (U.N.) is an organization that supports world peace. In 1999, the U.N. sent peacekeeping forces to Kosovo. This region is part of Serbia in the Federal Republic of Yugoslavia. Serbians did not want other groups of people to live in Kosovo. The U.N. wanted to protect people in this area from attacks by Serbian forces. U.S. troops were part of this mission.

The mission was dangerous. On March 31, 1999, three U.S. soldiers were captured by the Serbians. The U.S. soldiers were beaten and held captive until early May.

In June 1999, the Serbian forces began to leave Kosovo. People then were allowed to return to the area. Some U.N. peacekeeping forces stayed to help keep peace.

During the fighting, many roads and buildings had been destroyed in Kosovo. Army members helped rebuild roads and schools. Army members also provided medical care to people in Kosovo. Children received toothbrushes, candy, sunglasses, and stuffed animals from soldiers.

M1A1 Abrams Tank

Function: Main battle tank

Date Deployed: 1978

Speed: 45 miles (72 kilometers) per hour

Height: 8 feet (2.4 meters)

Weight: 54 tons (49 metric tons)

Main gun: 120 mm cannon

The M1A1 also has two 7.62 mm machine guns and one 12.7 mm machine gun.

The Abrams M1A1 is a fast and powerful tank. It is covered with heavy armor. These metal plates help protect tank operators. The tank also is made to protect troops from chemical weapons. It has a system that cleans the air tank operators breathe. The driver of an M1A1 looks out through a thermal viewer. This opening allows the driver to see objects even at night.

Almost all armor units in the Gulf War used M1A1 tanks. These tanks were painted the color of sand during the Gulf War. This coloring made it difficult for enemy forces to see them. About 2,000 M1A1 tanks were used during the Gulf War. Only 18 of these tanks were taken out of service because of damage.

The Army has worked on improvements to the M1A1. Currently, the M1A2 Abrams tank is the Army's main battle tank.

CHAPTER 4

Learn about:

- Comanche helicopter

- Women in the Army

- Army Rangers

The Army needs modern equipment to perform its missions.

Today's Army

Most U.S. military leaders doubt that there will be a major war in the near future. They expect the Army to be involved in smaller conflicts such as those in Somalia and Kosovo.

The Army currently performs four times as many missions as it did in the early 1990s. The Army needs modern equipment to perform these missions. The Army also needs to train its members for these missions.

New Equipment

The Army continues to need new equipment. The Crusader artillery system and the Comanche helicopter are examples of new equipment.

The Crusader artillery system includes two vehicles. One vehicle carries supplies such as fuel and ammunition. The second vehicle has a 155 mm howitzer. This large gun can hit targets up to 25 miles (40 kilometers) away. Crusaders can fire faster and farther than other artillery vehicles. They also can travel faster than most other military vehicles. Crusaders can reach speeds of 45 miles (72 kilometers) per hour on paved roads. They can travel 30 miles (48 kilometers) per hour off road.

The Comanche helicopter is designed for reconnaissance missions. Troops on these missions gather information about enemy forces. The Comanche allows troops to gather information during the day, night, or bad weather. Night vision goggles and radar allow Comanche crews to fly during most conditions. Night vision goggles allow pilots to see at night. Radar uses radio waves to locate distant objects.

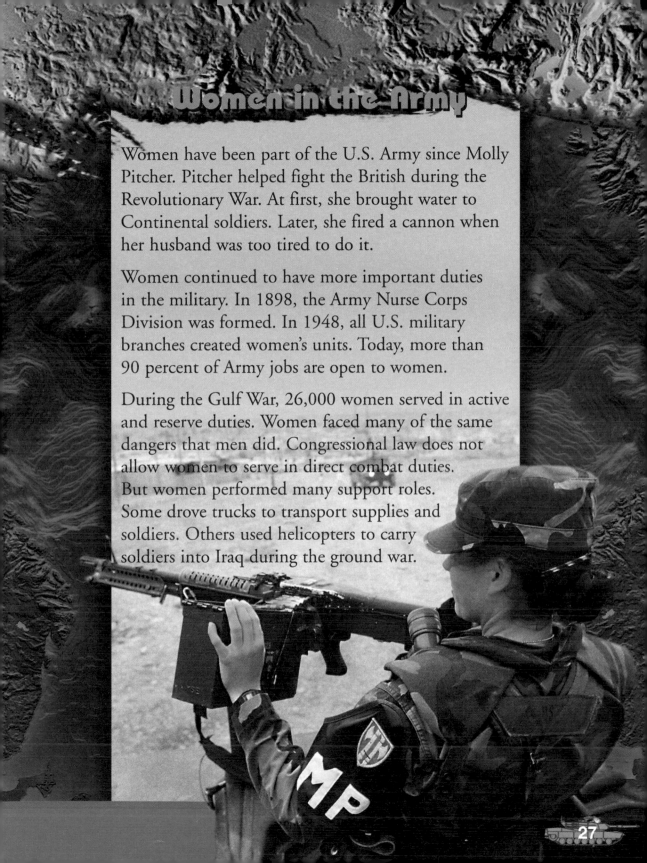

Women in the Army

Women have been part of the U.S. Army since Molly Pitcher. Pitcher helped fight the British during the Revolutionary War. At first, she brought water to Continental soldiers. Later, she fired a cannon when her husband was too tired to do it.

Women continued to have more important duties in the military. In 1898, the Army Nurse Corps Division was formed. In 1948, all U.S. military branches created women's units. Today, more than 90 percent of Army jobs are open to women.

During the Gulf War, 26,000 women served in active and reserve duties. Women faced many of the same dangers that men did. Congressional law does not allow women to serve in direct combat duties. But women performed many support roles. Some drove trucks to transport supplies and soldiers. Others used helicopters to carry soldiers into Iraq during the ground war.

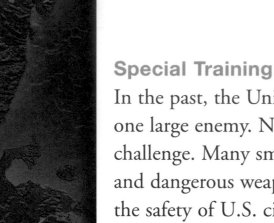

Special Training

In the past, the United States prepared to fight one large enemy. Now, the Army faces a new challenge. Many smaller nations have powerful and dangerous weapons. Terrorists also threaten the safety of U.S. citizens. Terrorists may kidnap people or make bomb threats for

Soldiers wear special clothing to protect themselves against chemical and biological weapons.

political reasons. Army members need special training to defend the United States against these situations.

Army members also prepare for the danger of biological and chemical weapons. Biological weapons contain germs that spread deadly diseases. Chemical weapons contain deadly poisons. Terrorists and some world governments may use these weapons. Army members wear special suits, masks, and boots to protect themselves against these weapons.

Army Rangers perform special missions. These soldiers train for special duties. Rangers often perform reconnaissance missions. They sneak into enemy areas to gather information about enemy forces. This information helps Army leaders plan missions. Army Rangers helped capture warlords in Somalia. They also train to prevent terrorist attacks.

U.S. Army members continue to prepare for future conflicts around the world. Special training and equipment helps Army members defend the United States.

Words to Know

allies (AL-eyes)—people, groups, or countries that work together for a common cause

enlisted member (en-LIST-id MEM-bur)—a member of the Army who is not an officer

officer (OF-uh-sur)—an Army member who directs enlisted members in their duties

parachute (PA-ruh-shoot)—a large piece of strong, lightweight fabric; parachutes allow soldiers to jump from airplanes and land safely on the ground.

paratrooper (PA-ruh-troo-pur)—a soldier trained to parachute

radar (RAY-dar)—a device that uses radio waves to locate objects

satellite (SAT-uh-lite)—a spacecraft that orbits Earth

trench (TRENCH)—a long, narrow ditch; soldiers fought in trenches during World War I.

To Learn More

Green, Michael. *The United States Army.* Serving Your Country. Mankato, Minn.: Capstone High-Interest Books, 1998.

Kent, Zachary. *The Persian Gulf War: "The Mother of All Battles."* American War. Hillside, N.J.: Enslow Publishers, 1994.

Scheafer, Silvia Anne. *Women in America's Wars.* Collective Biographies. Springfield, N.J.: Enslow Publishers, 1996.

Useful Addresses

U.S. Army Military History Institute
22 Ashburn Drive, Carlisle Barracks
Carlisle, PA 17013-5008

U.S. Army Public Affairs
Office of the Chief of Public Affairs
1500 Army Pentagon
Washington, DC 20310-1500

Internet Sites

ArmyLINK: U.S. Army Public Affairs

http://www.dtic.mil/armylink

U.S. Army

http://www.army.mil

U.S. Army Center of Military History

http://www.army.mil/cmh-pg/default.htm

Index